John Lennon

YOUNG ROCK STAR

John Lennon

YOUNG ROCK STAR

by Laurence Santrey
illustrated by Ellen Beier

Troll Associates

Library of Congress Cataloging-in-Publication Data

Santrey, Laurence.
    John Lennon: young rock star / by Laurence Santrey; illustrated by
Ellen Beier.
        p.   cm.
    Summary: A brief biography of the English rock musician with
emphasis on his early years and the formation of the famous Beatles.
    ISBN 0-8167-1781-8 (lib. bdg.)   ISBN 0-8167-1782-6 (pbk.)
    1. Lennon, John, 1940-1980—Juvenile literature.   2. Rock
musicians—England—Biography—Juvenile literature.   [1. Lennon,
John, 1940-1980—Childhood and youth.   2. Musicians.   3. Rock music.]
I. Beier, Ellen, ill.   II. Title.
ML3930.L34S26   1990
782.42166'092—dc20
    [B]   89-33938

John Lennon

YOUNG ROCK STAR

Bombs dropped from the black sky. They flashed white as they exploded. Ships, docks, and warehouses were blown to bits. Homes were on fire. Some people were hurt or dying. And some were already dead. Liverpool, England, was again being blasted by German bombers. It was October 9, 1940.

World War Two was raging in Europe. Nazi Germany seemed to be winning. Poland was defeated. Norway and Denmark were defeated. France surrendered. Country after country fell. And by the fall of 1940, Germany was trying to bomb Great Britain into giving up.

Hundreds of German warplanes flew across the English Channel. They dropped thousands of bombs on seaports, airfields, railway lines, and military areas. As one of England's most important seaports, Liverpool was often attacked.

A bomb fell not far from the hospital on Oxford Street. Inside, Julia Lennon worried as she waited to give birth. Her husband, Alfred, was away. He was serving aboard a ship somewhere in the North Atlantic Ocean. Julia's family was worried, too. It was a dangerous time in England, especially for a mother-to-be.

Then, late in the afternoon of October 9th, Julia Lennon's child was born. It was a boy. Her sister, Mimi Smith, got the news by phone. She told the rest of the family.

"We were five girls in my family," Mimi Smith remembered, "and I nearly went off my nut. I said, 'Mother, Mother, a boy, a boy! A boy in the family at last!'"

Mimi Smith rushed out of her house and ran toward the hospital. It was now evening, a time when the bombing raids usually started again. No buses were running. No traffic moved in the street. Hardly any people were out.

Sirens wailed as another raid began. Mimi kept on running. She ducked into doorways to avoid being hit. Then, during a break in the bombing, she raced the last few blocks to the hospital.

Moments later, she was in her sister's room. There, snuggled against his mother, was a beautiful baby boy. "We're going to call him John Winston," Julia told Mimi. "Isn't he lovely?"

Mimi Smith picked up the baby and held him close. Just then, a shrill siren announced another wave of bombers. A nurse hurried into the room and said visitors must leave. At the same time, she took baby John and placed him under his mother's bed. For newborn babies, this was the only protection the hospital had against flying glass and falling plaster.

Even when the bombs didn't drop, life was a struggle for Julia Lennon and her baby boy. Because of the war, food and clothing were sometimes hard to get. And money was another problem for Julia. She rarely had enough. For a short time, Alfred Lennon sent home some of his military pay. But Julia and her newborn son could not live on it. She had to go to work.

Julia did not have much education. Nor did she have any job training. That meant she could get only a very low-paying job. And so she took one as an usher in a movie theater. She also worked behind the candy counter.

While Julia worked, little John was looked after by Aunt Mimi. That was just wonderful for Mimi and her husband, George, a dairy farmer. They had no children of their own, and they adored their bright little nephew. Mimi loved taking John shopping and for walks in the park.

John had shining blond hair and bright eyes. He looked just like his mother. Julia and Mimi also looked very much alike. So the little boy also looked like Aunt Mimi. People who saw them together thought John was Mimi's son. That pleased her so much that she never bothered to tell them the truth. After a while, John thought of Aunt Mimi as a second mother.

At first, John spent weekdays with the Smiths. Weekends and nights, he was with his mother. But sometimes the weather was bad or Julia had to work late. And sometimes John had a cold. Then he would stay with his aunt and uncle. As time went on, he was staying less with his mother and more with his aunt and uncle.

13

Mimi and George gave John a great deal of love. Even so, it was confusing for him. Sometimes he lived in one place, sometimes in another. The youngster never knew where he would be from one day to the next.

Most of all, John missed having a father. Alfred Lennon did spend months at sea. But he could have come home several times, and he didn't. This was something John Lennon never talked about as he grew up.

The young John Lennon saw his father only once. John was five years old at the time. Alfred Lennon suddenly returned to Liverpool for a visit. He asked Julia if he could take John away for a few days. Alfred said that it would be nice for father and son to get to know each other. He wanted to take John to a friend's cottage in Blackpool, a popular place at the seashore. Julia wasn't sure, but she said yes.

Alfred and John were in Blackpool for two days when Julia came to their cottage. She wanted to take John back home. Alfred said no. He said he was going to leave England the next day and wanted to take John with him. Julia was angry, and there was a big argument. Then Julia and Alfred decided there was only one way to settle the argument. They called John into the room.

When John first saw his mother and father together, he was very happy. He had always dreamed of having a real family, all under the same roof. Then his dream was crushed. They told him he had to choose between Mommy and Daddy.

John was mixed up and sad. He looked at one parent, then at the other. At last, he whispered, "I'll stay with Daddy." Julia asked him if he was sure. John nodded.

Julia bent down and kissed John. Then she left.
When she was almost at the end of the street, she
heard "Mommy! Mommy! I changed my mind!"
John ran to his mother and threw himself into
her arms. They returned to Liverpool together.

On the trip back to Liverpool, Julia Lennon
made a big decision. She knew her son needed a
secure home. John also needed people who would
be there all the time. Julia could only be a part-
time parent. Aunt Mimi and Uncle George could
be with him day and night. And they wanted
John to live with them permanently.

From that day on, John Lennon lived full-time with the Smiths. Their home was a nice one, in a quiet suburb called Woolton. John had his own bedroom, facing the Smiths' garden. He spent many happy hours in his room. He liked to read, draw, and listen to the radio. Even as a young boy, John showed talent.

Aunt Mimi proudly remembered that John started to read when he was less than five years old. She told how he sat on his uncle's knee every evening. George read the local newspaper aloud, and the boy listened. Together, they spelled out the words in the headlines.

John learned to read this way. He also liked newspapers. For the rest of his life, he read as many newspapers as he could every day. This habit of reading helped John to learn many facts. He used a lot of these facts in the songs he wrote for the Beatles. For example, one of John's songs, "A Day in the Life," mentions "4,000 holes in Blackburn, Lancashire." They were the number of street potholes John had read about in a local British newspaper.

John Lennon wrote songs about love and peace, war and politics, and everything else that interested him. The poetry of his songs' lyrics came from the places and memories of his childhood. John's song "Strawberry Fields Forever," for example, was based on a real place. Right around the corner from John's house in Liverpool was Strawberry Field. It was a Salvation Army home for orphaned children.

Every summer, there was a carnival in the Strawberry Field garden. Aunt Mimi took John there. They had ice-cream cones and played carnival games. John loved the memories of going to carnivals with Aunt Mimi. His song captures forever the feelings of those childhood days.

Today, there is a place in America called Strawberry Fields. It is in New York City's Central Park. It is right across the street from the building where John lived his last years. Yoko Ono, John's widow, helped create this lovely garden in his memory. Many people visit Strawberry Fields every year.

When John was five years old, he entered primary school. Aunt Mimi was very careful to find the "right" one for her bright little nephew. She visited several schools before picking Dovedale Primary School. It was three miles from their home. To get there, John took a bus that went past Strawberry Field. It let him off on Penny Lane. "Penny Lane" is the title of another very popular Beatles song.

John was unusual even at the age of five. The Dovedale headmaster, Mr. Bolt, saw that right away. At the first parents' meeting, he said to Mimi, "There's no need to worry about John. He's sharp as a needle. But he won't do anything he doesn't want to." What Mr. Bolt said was perfectly true.

Schoolmates who remembered John years later described him as being special. One classmate said that "John was on a different wavelength from the others." Another classmate remembered John as "an oddball." But he added that John was looked up to by the others.

Most of the children admired John's cartoons, poems, and jokes. They enjoyed the clever new games he made up. And they praised him for his musical talents. John had a harmonica that he played all the time. He never took any formal music lessons. Everything John knew about music was what he taught himself.

There were two things about Dovedale that John did not like. One was the school uniform. All the students had to wear a black woolen jacket with a dove sewed on the pocket. The boys also had to wear a cap, gray short pants, knee socks, and a tie. John thought the jacket and tie were the worst of it. So he wore them in the sloppiest way he could. But he did wear them in order to keep out of trouble.

John also disliked the food served in the school lunchroom. So he did not hand in his lunch money to the teacher, as he was supposed to. Instead, he and a few friends went to Penny Lane for lunch. There, they bought cakes and other goodies. Many years later, John confessed to Aunt Mimi how he spent the lunch money she gave him.

In his years at Dovedale, John never seemed to study hard. But he really did a lot more school-work than he let his friends know. It was important to John to have the other kids believe he was tough. He wanted them to think he didn't care about anything. The truth was, he cared about a lot of things. It hurt him deeply when he was teased about not having a father around. It bothered him that he was terrible at arithmetic. He wanted to be the best at everything, but he didn't want anyone to know it.

John was able to hide how smart he was for a while. But the truth came out in 1951 when he had to take an important test. British school-children take a test when they are 11 years old. This test is called "the 11-plus." Students who do very well on the test can go on to a grammar school. In Britain, a grammar school is an upper school for top-level students. Children who do not pass the 11-plus go on to a less difficult kind of school. Only a small number of students pass the 11-plus each year. John did more than just pass the test. He did extremely well on it. That showed he had been working hard all along.

Something 11-year-old John really wanted was a fine bicycle, the kind the older boys rode. Uncle George knew this, and he promised John the bicycle if he passed the 11-plus. Uncle George loved John very much, and he also knew how bright the boy was. So Uncle George bought the bicycle months before John took the test. It was hidden in the house. Then, when the excited youngster came home with the good news, Uncle George said, "I have a surprise for you. It's outside. Why don't you look there?"

John rushed outside and found a shiny, bright green bicycle. Shouting "Thanks!" over his shoulder, John sped off on his marvelous gift. He couldn't wait to show it to his friends. It was the best present young John ever got.

In September 1952, John entered Quarry Bank Grammar School. He told his aunt and uncle he was looking forward to having a "smashing good time" and to learning a lot. Quarry Bank had a fine reputation. It was a hard school, but many of its boys went on to the top universities in Great Britain. As John found out, it was hard in more ways than just schoolwork.

Quarry Bank was an all-boys' school. Most of the teachers had been in military service during World War Two. They treated the students like new soldiers. The rules were very strict. Any boy who broke them was punished. Punishment could mean just being kept after school. But more often it was "caning."

A boy who was to be caned reported to the headmaster's office. There, the headmaster hit the student's hand with a stick. The number of hits depended on what the boy had done. At Quarry Bank, boys were caned for being late, looking sloppy, being fresh, and talking out of turn in class, among other offenses.

There was one rule that especially bothered John. The boys had to do every lesson and solve every problem in only one way. That was the teacher's way. If they thought of a different way to do the work, they were almost always caned for it. John was really creative and different. This kept getting him into trouble—and into the headmaster's office for caning.

Something else about Quarry Bank bothered
John a lot. The boys were divided into five groups
for sports and other activities. The groups were
called "houses." This was how Quarry Bank
copied England's finest upper-class boarding
schools. At boarding schools, students live in
different houses. Each house has its own teams,
which play against teams of other houses.

At Quarry Bank, the boys didn't live at school. They went home every day. So they were grouped in "houses" according to the neighborhood where they lived. That way, the boys from the richest neighborhood were kept together. The boys from the poorest neighborhood were kept together. And all those in-between were separated in the same way.

John Lennon's house at Quarry Bank was called Woolton, for the neighborhood where he lived. It was a middle-class group because Woolton was a middle-class neighborhood. John liked most of the boys in his group. What he objected to was the system of separation. He felt it was wrong to divide the boys according to their family incomes. He didn't believe that rich boys were any better than poor boys.

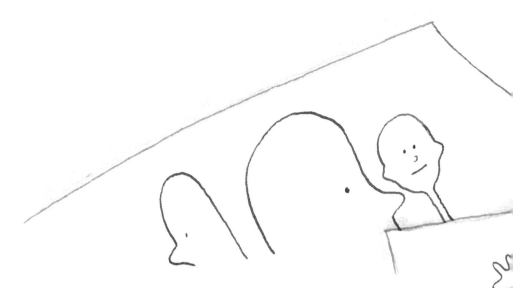

John wasn't afraid to show how he felt. He spoke up about the way school sports were run, even though it got him into trouble. Sports were important at Quarry Bank, but not simply for the fun of playing. Winning was what mattered. Boys who didn't do well at sports were laughed at. John thought this was unfair, and he refused to take part in school sports.

When John saw that the boys with lower-class accents were being made fun of, he started to speak the way they did. Years later, some people were sure John Lennon came from the slums of Liverpool because of the way he talked. He didn't let them know he was using the accent he picked up in his Quarry Bank days.

English and art were John's best subjects at
Quarry Bank. He wrote poetry and short stories
that showed great imagination. He also drew
many cartoons that were wild and funny. In his
other classes, he did not do well at all. It wasn't
that he didn't care about school. John was very
nearsighted, and he could not see the blackboard.
But he didn't say anything about it.

Nothing was done until Aunt Mimi took John for an eye test. The test showed that he had very poor eyesight. At first, John did not want to wear eyeglasses. But he gave in when he understood how important eyeglasses were. In his years as a Beatle, John was famous for wearing different styles of eyeglasses. And whatever style of eyeglasses he wore was soon worn by thousands of his fans.

During his Quarry Bank years, from the ages of 12 to 17, many changes took place in John Lennon's life. His loving uncle George died suddenly in 1955. George Smith had been a true father to John, and the teen-ager felt a great loss at his death. John's unhappiness grew worse three years later. His mother was struck and killed by a swerving car as she walked across a road.

As a teen-ager, John always wanted to be close with his mother. He used to visit her after school and on weekends. Around this time, John started to play the guitar. He also liked to play rock records. This music bothered Aunt Mimi, but Julia Lennon enjoyed it as much as John did. She told him the music he listened to and played was fantastic!

In 1956, John and his friends formed their first band, the Quarry Men. Julia was their biggest fan. She didn't act like a mother to John. She was a friend who never told him what to do, and she didn't try to change the way he acted.

Julia Lennon was different from the other adults John knew. In those days, most women did not wear trousers. Julia did. She dressed and talked without worrying about what other people thought. John, the young rebel, saw himself as his mother's son. He also dressed, talked, and acted the way he wanted to. So his mother's death was a cruel blow to 17-year-old John.

After his mother died, John went into a shell. He didn't talk much about her. But there was one friend, a member of the Quarry Men, who understood John's pain and loss. He was Paul McCartney. Paul's mother had died two years earlier. Lennon and McCartney had two strong bonds—their music and their grief. In time, the grief passed. But their music continued to grow. And ten years after her death, John and Paul would write a song together, "Julia," in memory of John's mother.

Aunt Mimi wanted John to pay more attention to school and less attention to his music. She hoped he would work hard at Quarry Bank Grammar School and go on to a university. "The guitar is all very well, John," she said. "But you'll never make a *living* out of it."

John didn't want to give up music. He asked Mimi to let him work at it a bit longer—"to get it out of my system." Mimi agreed. She still hoped John would see that there wasn't much future in playing a guitar.

Music was too important for John to give up. He stayed with it, and his schoolwork did not improve. There was no chance that any university would accept him. Still, his grades were good enough to get him into the Liverpool College of Art in 1957. John's talent as an artist was clear to his teachers and classmates. But music was taking over his life.

John Lennon and Paul McCartney practiced together for hours and hours. They also began composing songs together. The Quarry Men played at local dances, youth clubs, and any place else they could find an audience. The band was made up of three guitar players and one drummer. Early in 1958, a new guitar player joined John and Paul as a regular. His name was George Harrison.

The teen-agers played together for two years. In that time, they got better and better. And the group's name changed a number of times. "The Quarry Men," "Johnny and the Moondogs," "the Rainbows," and "the Silver Beatles" were some of the names used.

Where did the name "Beatles" come from? A band member jokingly suggested they call themselves "Beetles." It was a kind of tribute to American rock star Buddy Holly's band, the Crickets. Someone else suggested using a famous pirate's name from *Treasure Island*, Long John Silver. The two were combined into "Long John and the Silver Beatles." But John Lennon didn't want to be called "Long John," so that part was dropped. "The Silver Beatles," however, stuck. And after a while, it was shortened to just "the Beatles."

In 1960, the band played their first professional job as the Beatles. The band was now John, Paul, George, bass player Stu Sutcliffe, and drummer Pete Best. Stu Sutcliffe, an art school friend of John's, left the group in 1961 to paint. A year after that, Pete Best was replaced by Ringo Starr. John, Paul, George, and Ringo were the four who went on to fame and fortune as the Beatles.

At first, the Beatles played in small nightclubs and at local dances. But soon they were hired to play in other British cities. They even played in Hamburg, West Germany. As they got better and better, the Beatles earned more money and worked at larger clubs. They played less and less music written by other rock composers. More and more, they were playing songs written by themselves, especially by Lennon and McCartney.

The 1960s have been called the "Decade of the Beatles." Their songs were played all over the world. Hits such as "Yellow Submarine," "Yesterday," "All You Need Is Love," and dozens of others are still played. Their movies—*A Hard Day's Night, Help!* and *Yellow Submarine*—were seen by millions of eager fans. John, Paul, George, and Ringo became very rich.

By the late 1960s, the Beatles started to drift
apart. In 1969, the year of their largest album
sales, they almost broke up. And in 1970, they did.
Each of them wanted to do different things with
his life. John and his wife, Yoko Ono, recorded
albums of their own music. John also wrote books,
which had his own drawings. And he began
painting again. For a while, he dropped out of
music entirely, giving his time completely to
Yoko and their son, Sean.

In 1980, the Lennons started to record a new album. It was never completed. Late on the night of December 8, 1980, John Lennon was killed in front of his New York City home. A few hours later, people started to gather across from the Lennons' home. Many held candles in their hands, the small flames flickering in the cold night air. Well into the morning, they stood and softly sang John's songs. And that same day, millions of others mourned his death around the world.

John Lennon is gone. But the music he made is not. It is still popular, still being recorded, still finding new listeners. As John's widow, Yoko, said, "His spirit is in the world forever."